SHADES OF RESILIENCE

THE SKIN I'M IN

No part of this publication may be reproduced in any form, stored in any retrieval system, posted on any website, or transmitted in any form or by any means – digital, electronic, scanning, photocopy, recording, or otherwise without written permission from the author.

This book is fiction. This book's characters, places, and events are fictitious products of the author's imagination. Any resemblance or similarity to real people, living or dead, companies, institutions, organizations, or incidents is entirely coincidental and not intended by the author.

Copyright © 2023 by Tanisha Buxton-Banks

ISBN: 978-0-996-1862-9-2

All rights reserved. Copyright infringement is a serious offense.

RBMB Publishing at
RBMB1263@yahoo.com
"The Other Side of Alzheimer's, a caregiver's story"
"The Gospel Choir Murder"
"Thou Shalt Kill"
"Murder without a home"

Printed in the United States of America

Preface

In crafting this book about Vitiligo, I embark on a journey to illuminate the complexities of this skin condition. I intend to bring awareness with narratives, fostering a deeper understanding of Vitiligo's impact. Through these pages, I hope to contribute to the knowledge surrounding Vitiligo and the empathy and support crucial for those navigating its challenges. I see you, I hear you, I am you.

This book is dedicated to

Janice Buxton

"You are the guiding light of my life, my dearest Mother, whose love is my unwavering anchor and strength is my greatest inspiration."

****

And Angie

For your support, that illuminated my path. Your assistance made this journey possible.

Thank you,

Angie

SHADES OF RESILIENCE

Poem
"THE SKIN I'M IN"
Written by Tanisha Buxton-Banks

I love the skin I'm in.
My perfect imperfection, I'ma teach you a lesson, but I have just one question. Why me? Or rather, why not me?
The skin I'm in has taught me resilience.
Resilience: the ability to rebound or recover from disappointment.
Can I get some ointment?
To treat this visual phenomenon.
No, there is no cure for the skin I'm in; it is a permanent realization I have to endure.
Vitiligo, they call it. Michael Jackson had it too. But the public shunned him; they didn't have a clue.
Vitiligo is a skin disorder caused by the destruction of cells, making blotches on my skin, the color of seashells.
I wear it with Grace, even though it spreads all over my face.
I would not have known my own strength if I didn't have to bounce back from what started as a pin-sized mark under my eye.
Resilience, refusing to give up or give into my circumstance, shall we dance?
To a different drum. I'm different, yeah I'm different, I'm different, Yeah I'm different.
I am different, as you see, but I'm OK with it because it's just me.
I don't mind the stares, and I don't fall for the gloom
I'm that silent elephant in the room. You can see it on the outside, but the inside is to blame
My question?
Can you see what's inside of you when you're wearing your shame?
Some people don't see it cause my persona plays tricks with your psyche or possibly a temporary blindness from something so obvious, yet to the people who love me, it seems to go unnoticed.
I don't have the money like Michael to even out with speed.

SHADES OF RESILIENCE

I wear my shame for the whole world to see, but I don't let it stop me.
Stop me from teaching, stop me from living, stop me from loving and such.
Resilience, they call it, and snapback, I must.

Misha

A 21-year-old woman named Misha lives in Saint Louis, MO, a city known for its vibrant culture and rich diversity. Misha is a college graduate, a confident and ambitious woman who embraces her heritage. Her personality and outgoing spirit attract friends of all ethnicities. Her talent as a photographer and painter showcases beauty from within. With her radiant dark skin, Misha moves through life with grace and determination.

While preparing for a special event one sunny afternoon, Misha saw her reflection in the mirror. Surprisingly, she noticed a small patch of skin on the back of her arm that appeared lighter than the rest. Curiosity sparked within her as she wondered what could have caused this sudden change. Concerned yet intrigued, Misha decided to seek medical advice. Weeks later, she visited a renowned dermatologist specializing in various skin conditions.

The doctor carefully examined her skin and confirmed that she had Vitiligo, which causes skin pigmentation loss. According to the doctor, this spot could spread over her body. Misha felt mixed emotions – confusion, sadness, and fear. Because her skin was so dark, there was no way she could hide whiter spots on her skin. Misha has always been careful not to get sunburned and has no health issues. She questioned why this happened to her but soon realized that dwelling on self-pity would not change her circumstances. With her strong-willed nature, she faced this new chapter head-on, determined to learn more about Vitiligo and find self-acceptance.

Misha embarked on a journey of self-discovery, seeking knowledge about Vitiligo and connecting with others who shared similar experiences. She discovered a supportive community of individuals who embraced their unique skin patterns and saw beauty in their differences. Inspired by their resilience, Misha found solace and strength. Eager to spread awareness and change the narrative surrounding Vitiligo, Misha decided to use her voice and platform to educate others.

She began sharing her journey on social media, sharing her vulnerability and empowering others to embrace their unique skin journeys. Her posts garnered attention and admiration, resonating with people from all walks of life. As Misha continued to embrace her individuality, she also found solace in fashion and beauty.

She became an advocate for representation, encouraging brands and designers to include models with Vitiligo in their campaigns and runway shows. Misha's confidence and unwavering determination began to shift societal perspectives, making strides toward inclusivity in the fashion industry. Through advocacy and openness, Misha became a symbol of strength and self-acceptance for women with Vitiligo. Her story spread far and wide, inspiring countless others to embrace their unique beauty and find strength in their differences. Over time, Misha's journey caught the attention of a renowned art curator who recognized the power of her story.

She showcased her journey through a series of captivating photographs and paintings, capturing the essence of her strength and resilience. The exhibition became a celebration of diversity and self-love, drawing people from all walks of life to experience the beauty of embracing one's unique journey. Misha felt a profound sense of accomplishment as she stood before her artwork.

Her journey of self-discovery and acceptance had not only transformed her own life but touched the lives of others. Misha realized that Vitiligo was not a burden but a gift that allowed her to inspire others and reshape societal beauty standards.

Her story became a powerful testament to the beauty and strength of women with Vitiligo. Her journey of self-love and acceptance paved the way for others to embrace their unique paths, reminding the world that true beauty lies in the diversity within us all.

SHADES OF RESILIENCE

Maya

Once upon a time, a 16-year-old girl named Maya lived in Mexico City. Maya is a gifted young dancer known for captivating and celebrating her culture's diversity and beauty in her dance. She had always been proud of her rich, melanin-filled skin, cherishing her Mexican heritage.

One sunny morning, while gathering her costume for a school event, Maya saw a strange spot on her face. Looking in the mirror, she observed a small patch of white, devoid of pigment, on her cheek. Confused and curious, she touched it gently, wondering what could have caused this change in her complexion. For weeks, the spot had been growing larger. Now, the scar on her cheek was the size of a pea and very noticeable.

Maya ran to her mother concerned. Her mother had no idea what could have caused the spot and decided to seek medical advice. The family doctor referred them to a dermatologist. After carefully examining Maya's skin and a series of tests and consultations, the doctor revealed that she had Vitiligo, which causes depigmentation in some skin regions. The dermatologist told her the spot on her cheek could spread.

The news took Maya aback. She had never heard of Vitiligo and could not imagine how it would affect her. Initially, she felt mixed emotions – confusion, sadness, and even shame with a hint of fear. What would her classmates think? Despite medication, the spot continued to expand. Some of her friends began to tease and bully her, causing her to feel worse about her appearance. Maya's dance teacher noticed she was becoming withdrawn. She no longer volunteered to participate in dance events. When she began to miss classes, her teacher became very concerned. When asked, Maya told her she was considering quitting dance because of her appearance. The teacher asked Maya to write a book report explaining her condition. Maya agreed. After reading her book report to the class, her classmates became compassionate and stopped teasing her.

Determined to learn even more about Vitiligo, Maya delved into research and connected with others older than her who were experiencing the same condition. She discovered people who celebrated their unique skin patterns and encouraged others to embrace their beauty.

Maya realized that dancing could be vital in spreading awareness and fostering acceptance. She began creating powerful dance routines showcasing diversity in beauty, including different skin tones and patterns. Her dancing became a source of inspiration for others with Vitiligo and a testament to the beauty within each unique individual.

Maya also started posting her story on social media, using her platform to educate and empower others. Her vulnerability and courage touched the hearts of many, creating a ripple effect of acceptance and understanding.

As she aged and the spot expanded, Maya's dancing gained recognition. Her powerful dance routines allowed her to join a famous dance company where she was the featured dancer. Maya's dancing became a symbol of inclusivity and a celebration of beauty.

As Maya's appearance changed with Vitiligo, she discovered that her uniqueness was not a limitation but a source of strength. Her journey of self-discovery and acceptance inspired others to embrace their individuality, no matter their differences.

Maya's story became a powerful testament to the resilience and beauty of people with Vitiligo—her journey of self-love and acceptance spread far and wide, reminding everyone that our differences make us truly beautiful.

Lily

Once upon a time, in a cozy house beside a vibrant meadow lived a compassionate and nurturing parent named Emily and her imaginative and inquisitive 11-year-old daughter named Lily. With her bright blue eyes and adventurous spirit, Lily was always eager to explore the world around her.

One sunny afternoon, while playing in the park, Lily noticed something unusual. She glanced at her leg and gasped in surprise. Small patches of her skin had lost their natural color, leaving behind a pale hue. She turned to her mother, Emily, her eyes wide with curiosity.

"Mom!" Lily exclaimed, "Look at my legs! Why are they changing color?"

Tender-hearted and wise, Emily kneeled beside Lily, placing her little shin on her lap. She was shocked. A spot on Lily's leg appeared whiter than her normal skin. Emily assured her daughter it wasn't a concern, but Lily was scared. Her family doctor referred her to a dermatologist 20 miles from where they lived. "My dear, he said, what you have discovered is called Vitiligo. It's a unique condition that affects the color of your skin. But let me assure you, it doesn't change anything about who you are."

Lily's brow furrowed with concern. She turned to her mother and said, "But Mom, will people think I'm strange or different now?"

Emily smiled gently, her voice soothing and reassuring. "Oh, my precious child, you are far from strange or different. You are even more extraordinary. Like a rainbow with its vibrant colors, your Vitiligo adds a touch of magic to your appearance."

Lily's eyes sparkled with curiosity. "Magic, Mom? How is that possible?"

Emily's voice carried a sense of wonder. "Yes, my darling. Your skin tells a story, a tale of uniqueness and courage. Each patch of color speaks of your strength and resilience. It's like having a secret treasure map on your skin, guiding you to embrace your beauty."

Lily looked at her hands, marveling at the patterns that had emerged. "So, Mom, this makes me special?"

Emily nodded, love radiating from her eyes. "My precious one. You are a masterpiece, a work of art, and your Vitiligo is like brush strokes on a canvas. It sets you apart in the most beautiful way."

Lily's worries faded, replaced by a newfound sense of pride. She started seeing her Vitiligo as a badge of honor, symbolizing her individuality. Her mother's guidance taught her to embrace her unique appearance and share her story with others.

As Lily grew older, she became an advocate for self-acceptance and diversity. Her confidence and kindness shone brightly, inspiring those around her to celebrate their differences. Lily spread love, understanding, and the beauty of uniqueness.

Lily's journey with Vitiligo became a source of empowerment, reminding everyone that true beauty lies within. Her story touched the hearts of many, teaching them to appreciate the diverse tapestry of humanity and to cherish the beauty that lies in our differences.

Ultimately, Lily and Emily's bond grew closer, their love and support guiding them through any challenge. Lily's Vitiligo became a part of her identity, a reminder to embrace her unique story and always find beauty in the world around her.

Jennifer

Jennifer is a single and successful 26-year-old criminal attorney living in New York City. At work, Jennifer is known for her infectious laughter, dynamic personality, and love for exploring new things. But for almost two years, she's been living with a secret. She stopped dating even though she wanted love in her life.

One sunny day, as Jennifer strolled through a bustling marketplace, she noticed a small booth with a colorful array of face and body paints. Intrigued, she approached the booth, where a wise old artist named Amara sat with a warm smile on her face.

Amara's booth was full of stunning paintings, each telling its story. Jennifer couldn't help but be captivated by the unique artwork, which celebrated the beauty of diversity in all its forms. An overwhelming feeling of curiosity washed over her as she admired the paintings.

Unable to contain her excitement, Jennifer asked Amara, "What inspires you to create such beautiful art?"

Amara replied, her voice warmed, "I believe that true beauty lies in embracing our uniqueness, our differences. Each stroke of my paintbrush celebrates the diverse stories that make up our world."

Jennifer's eyes widened with wonder as she shared her story with Amara. She explained how she was diagnosed with Vitiligo. It started with patches on her stomach and has been spreading over her body. Her skin gives her a unique and unfamiliar appearance. Ashamed of her body, she stopped dating.

SHADES OF RESILIENCE

Amara's eyes sparkled with understanding as she gently exclaimed, "Ah, my dear, it seems you have discovered the beautiful journey of Vitiligo!"

Jennifer's curiosity grew more intense, and she leaned closer, eager to learn more.

Amara continued, "As you know, Vitiligo is a condition that affects the pigmentation of the skin, creating striking patterns and variations. It is a canvas upon which your life's story showcases the beauty of your individuality." Amara lifted her blouse to review that she also had Vitiligo.

Jennifer's heart swelled with a newfound appreciation for her condition. She realized that Vitiligo is something you can't hide from but rather a unique part of her life's story waiting to be shared.

Inspired by Amara's words, Jennifer decided to celebrate her Vitiligo creatively. She started by renewing her gym membership. Her first class was scary because she didn't know how others would react to her appearance. Her workout attire showed the areas of her skin that were different. To her surprise, no one stared or asked why her skin looked different. Weeks later, a young man started a conversation. She was surprised when he asked her out for a date. Months later, during a conversation, Jennifer asked him why he had never asked her about her skin condition.

His answer shocked her. "At first, I was afraid to ask you out because clearly, you are a strong and beautiful woman who is not superficial. Whatever happens with your body, you honor the beauty of your uniqueness. I admire you for that." Jennifer told him about her condition and thanked him for recognizing her true strength. The conversation convinced her to share her story with colleagues.

SHADES OF RESILIENCE

Word of Jennifer's condition spread around the office. She no longer hid the fact that Vitiligo had spread to her arms. Jennifer's journey of self-discovery and celebration of her Vitiligo transformed her life and touched the hearts of those around her. In embracing her uniqueness, she helped others find the courage to embrace their stories and live authentically. Jennifer married the man who accepted her for her inner beauty and strength.

So, Jennifer's vibrant spirit became a testament to the power of self-love, acceptance, and the beauty within our differences. Her story reminds us that we are all beautifully unique, and our true beauty shines when we embrace our individuality.

Shahid Farid

Shahid Farid was born in Mardan, a small city in Pakistan. As a brilliant student, he aspired to become a doctor in America. His parents and relatives were so proud when he received a scholarship from a prestigious college in Boston, MA. He excelled and soon graduated with honors, and his residency was to be at a local hospital. As an international student, Shahid took pride in his appearance, especially since he was studying to be a dermatologist. His rich, melanin-filled skin was flawless.

He was in his second year when he noticed a small patch of white devoid of pigment on his cheek. He touched it gently, hoping it was not Vitiligo, a condition he knew about in college.

While he knew about Vitiligo, there was no definitive reason why it happened, and none of his colleagues specialized in researching this condition. Shahid was heartbroken. He knew the spot on his face would enlarge and never imagined Vitiligo would affect him.

He felt mixed emotions – confusion, sadness, disappointment, and fear. How could he be a successful dermatologist and face patients with Vitiligo on his face? Over time, Shahid became depressed and decided to give up his dream, leave America, and return home. But before making a final decision, he heard about a research study on skin conditions at another hospital. Reluctantly, Shahid decided to attend the conference and listened to presentations, but no one mentioned research on Vitiligo.

Shahid knew he wasn't the only one affected by Vitiligo and other skin problems. So, he decided to focus his practice on helping patients with skin conditions without a cure.

Yes, his face changed, but to his surprise, patients accepted him because of his condition. Seeing him gave them comfort, knowing he knew how they felt, having a skin condition that is noticeable to everyone. It gave them the confidence to share their story.

Shahid provides his patients with a pamphlet he wrote, encouraging them to use their platform to educate and empower others. He has touched the hearts of many, creating a ripple effect of acceptance and understanding, and for them to see the beauty in who they are. Vitiligo did not stop him from being the best doctor he could be.

SHADES OF RESILIENCE

Nia

In the vibrant city of Harlem, a young and talented artist named Nia lived. She was passionate about painting and spent hours in her studio, bringing her colorful imagination to life on canvas. Her dark skin, rich like the night sky, was a source of pride for her, representing her African heritage and resilience.

One summer morning, while Nia was preparing for an art exhibition, she noticed a small patch of her skin on her hand had turned stark white. Confusion and concern washed over her, and she wondered what could have caused this sudden change. Nia sought answers from a knowledgeable dermatologist specializing in various skin conditions.

Nia's heart raced with anticipation at the doctor's office as she awaited her examination. The dermatologist carefully inspected her skin. She had Vitiligo, which causes skin pigmentation loss. Initially, she felt surprise, sadness, fear, and worried about how the world would perceive her, especially as an artist whose work often reflected her image.

However, as days passed, Nia's perspective began to shift. She realized that her worth as an artist and as a person extended far beyond the boundaries of her skin. With determination, Nia embraced her new journey, using her art to express her emotions and spread awareness about Vitiligo.

Nia painted a self-portrait, capturing the contrast between her dark skin and the white patch that now adorned her hand. The painting portrayed her journey of self-discovery and acceptance, showcasing the beauty and strength that lay within her unique canvas. She named the piece "Shades of Resilience" and displayed it at her art exhibition.

SHADES OF RESILIENCE

To her surprise, "Shades of Resilience" resonated deeply with the viewers. People from all walks of life marveled at how Nia had transformed her perceived flaw into a work of art that celebrated her individuality. Nia's painting sparked conversations about beauty standards and embracing differences.

News of Nia's artwork spread like wildfire, catching the attention of a prominent fashion magazine. The magazine reached out to her, inviting her to collaborate on a special edition celebrating diversity in beauty. Excited about the opportunity to challenge societal norms, she eagerly accepted.

Nia and the magazine's team curated a stunning photoshoot featuring models of diverse backgrounds, including those with Vitiligo. Each photograph highlighted the unique beauty and resilience of the models and aimed to redefine the fashion industry's narrow standards of beauty. The issue became a sensation, inspiring countless individuals to embrace their uniqueness.

As Nia's artwork and advocacy gained recognition, she became a voice for black women with Vitiligo, empowering them to love themselves unconditionally. She started hosting workshops and speaking engagements where she shared her story and encouraged others to find strength in their differences.

Through her journey, Nia realized that her Vitiligo was not a hindrance but a gift that allowed her to connect with others on a deeper level. She understood that true beauty is within one's spirit, talent, and ability to embrace and celebrate their individuality.

Nia's discovery of Vitiligo became a catalyst for change, not only in her own life but in the lives of many others. Her art and advocacy broke down barriers, inspiring a new era of inclusivity and acceptance in art and beauty. Nia's courage and resilience taught the world that true beauty lies in embracing and celebrating the unique shades of our existence.

Ethan

A loving father named David and his courageous son, Ethan, lived in a quaint neighborhood by a peaceful lake. With his contagious laughter and gentle heart, Ethan possessed a rare beauty that captivated those around him. However, his journey was not without its challenges, for Ethan carried the burden of being bullied due to his Vitiligo.

One sunny morning, as David prepared breakfast, he noticed a sadness on Ethan's face. Ethan was quiet. His eyes were downcast, his shoulders hunched as if carrying the world's weight upon them. Perceptive and empathetic, David recognized the pain etched upon his son's expression.

Putting a plate of warm pancakes before Ethan, David gently sat beside him. "Son, I see the sadness in your eyes; tell me, what troubles your heart today?"

Ethan sighed, his voice tinged with vulnerability. "Dad, the kids in school keep teasing me because of my Vitiligo. They call me names and say hurtful things. I don't understand why they can't accept me for who I am."

David's heart ached for his son, but his eyes shone with determination. He reached out, placing a comforting hand on Ethan's shoulder. "My dear boy, I want you to know that their hurtful words do not define you. You are a remarkable young man with a spirit that shines brighter than the sun. Your Vitiligo is a part of you, but it is not what makes you special. Your kindness, resilience, and compassion set you apart."

Ethan looked up, his eyes searching for the truth in his father's words. "But Dad, it's hard. It hurts when they laugh and point at me."

David nodded, acknowledging Ethan's pain. "I understand, my son. It's difficult, but remember, their ignorance is not yours to bear. Instead, focus on educating them about Vitiligo and spreading kindness in the face of adversity."

Ethan's face brightened, his spirit rekindled by his father's unwavering support. "How can we do that, Dad?"

David smiled, a glimmer of pride in his eyes. "Together, we will rise above the hurtful words. We will share your story, strength, and courage with others to educate and inspire compassion."

David and Ethan embarked on a journey of empowerment and education. They organized presentations at Ethan's school, where they spoke about Vitiligo, its impact on individuals, and the need for acceptance and understanding. They shared anecdotes, shedding light on the beauty that lies within diversity.

As the days turned into weeks, a change began to stir within Ethan's school. Once fueled by ignorance, the bullies started to see the true character of their words. Slowly but surely, they realized the hurt they had caused and the strength within Ethan's spirit.

One by one, the bullies approached Ethan, their eyes filled with remorse. They offered heartfelt apologies, their words laced with newfound understanding and empathy. Ethan, embracing forgiveness and growth, welcomed them with open arms.

As the school year progressed, Ethan's courage and resilience became a beacon of hope for others facing adversity. His story touched the hearts of many, inspiring them to celebrate differences and embrace the uniqueness that makes each extraordinary.

Ultimately, Ethan's journey with Vitiligo transformed his perspective and ignited a shift in his community. David, proud of his son's strength and the love he had fostered within him, marveled at the power of compassion and education.

Together, father and son stood tall, their bond unbreakable. They had turned the darkness of bullying into a spark of enlightenment, turning ignorance into understanding and creating a world where kindness prevailed. And in their small corner of the world, they spread love and acceptance, one person at a time.

SHADES OF RESILIENCE

Miss Emily

In a small town nestled between city life and suburban Atlanta, there was a remarkable teacher named Miss Emily. She possessed an extraordinary gift for spreading knowledge, compassion, and joy among her students. Miss Emily's heartwarming smile lit up the room, and her laugh was infectious. However, something unique about Miss Emily caught her students' attention - she had Vitiligo, which caused patches of her skin to lose pigmentation.

One sunny morning, as the students filed into the classroom, whispers and curious glances filled the air. They had noticed Miss Emily's changing skin, and their innocent minds couldn't help but wonder. Sensing their curiosity, Miss Emily addressed the topic, turning it into a valuable lesson about acceptance and empathy.

Miss Emily gathered her students in a circle, "Good morning, my wonderful learners! Today, I want to share something special with all of you. You may have noticed the changes in my skin, and I want to explain what it's all about." The children listened intently, their eyes wide with curiosity.

"Have you ever seen a beautiful rainbow in the sky?" Miss Emily asked, and the children nodded in unison. "Well, just like a rainbow, we are unique and special. My skin is like a canvas, and the patches you see are like strokes of different colors on a painting."

Miss Emily continued, "Sometimes, our bodies express themselves differently like some people have different hair or eye colors. Vitiligo is a condition that affects the color of my skin, but it doesn't change who I am on the inside. Just like you, I have dreams, hopes, and feelings."

The children listened attentively, their faces reflecting curiosity and understanding. But Miss Emily knew that truly embracing diversity required more than just words. She decided to engage her students in a creative activity that would deepen their comprehension and empathy.

Miss Emily invited each student to create their unique masterpiece with colorful paints, brushes, and a big canvas. As the children excitedly mixed and blended colors, they experienced firsthand how beauty could emerge from diversity. Each stroke symbolized their understanding that differences should be celebrated rather than feared.

Once the paintings were complete, Miss Emily arranged them around the classroom, forming a gallery of diversity. The children admired their creations and marveled at how each piece was distinct and beautiful, just like their teacher.

From that day forward, the students viewed Miss Emily's Vitiligo not as something strange but as a reminder of the beauty within diversity. They learned to appreciate and accept each other's differences, fostering a classroom environment where kindness and understanding flourished.

Miss Emily's gentle guidance and creative approach taught her students about Vitiligo and awakened their hearts to the true essence of compassion and acceptance.

And every passing year, Miss Emily's classroom became a place where every child felt seen, understood, and loved for who they were.

SHADES OF RESILIENCE

The story of Miss Emily, the extraordinary teacher with Vitiligo, became a legend in that town. It also sparked Miss Emily to create a spoken word poem about her journey to share with the entire school, reminding generations of students that embracing diversity was the key to building a kinder and more inclusive world.

SHADES OF RESILIENCE

Alex

In San Francisco, there was a passionate and ambitious news anchor named Alex with a smile and a voice that captivated viewers. He had always dreamt of being a beacon of truth and inspiration in journalism.

Every day, Alex would arrive at the news station ready to report on the latest events with utmost professionalism and dedication. However, one morning, something caught his eye while preparing in front of the mirror. A small patch of skin on his face had lost its pigmentation, leaving a striking contrast against the rest of his complexion.

Alex's heart skipped a beat, realizing that he had developed Vitiligo. Questions filled his mind, and a wave of uncertainty washed over him. Would this change jeopardize his career? Would the viewers still accept him as their trusted news anchor?

Though apprehensive, Alex bravely decided to face this new challenge head-on. He sought advice from a supportive dermatologist, who reassured him that Vitiligo does not define his abilities, intelligence, or talent. The makeup staff experimented with different techniques to address his Vitiligo. Skillfully, they blended shades and hues, turning his daily makeup routine into a canvas of creativity. Soon, viewers began to notice the stunning transformations and the confidence that radiated from Alex's on-screen presence.

Embracing and accepting his unique condition, Alex shared his journey with his loved ones, colleagues, and, eventually, his viewers.

Word of Alex's inspiring story spread throughout the city,

touching the hearts of countless individuals who also faced personal challenges. They symbolized empowerment, showing that diversity should be celebrated and embraced in every aspect of life.

The news station, recognizing Alex's story's immense impact on his audience, dedicated a particular segment to raise awareness about Vitiligo and other skin conditions. Alex seized this opportunity to educate and encourage others, emphasizing that true strength lies in accepting and loving oneself, regardless of appearance.

As the days went by, Alex's journey continued to inspire and empower people from all walks of life. His name became synonymous with resilience, compassion, and unwavering determination. His newfound purpose paved the way for a more inclusive and accepting society, where differences are not obstacles but beautiful aspects that make each person unique.

Alex shared the latest headlines with each news report and reminded the world that true beauty comes from within and that we should embrace and celebrate the diversity surrounding us all.

What is Vitiligo?

Vitiligo is a chronic (long-lasting) autoimmune disorder that causes patches of skin to lose pigment or color. This condition happens when melanocytes — skin cells that make pigment — are attacked and destroyed, causing the skin to turn a milky-white color. Approximately 70 million people worldwide have Vitiligo. Vitiligo doesn't discriminate and is found to be relatively equal in all ethnicities and sexes.[1]

---

[1] https://www.mayoclinic.org/diseases-conditions/vitiligo/symptoms-causes/syc-20355912

www.ingramcontent.com/pod-product-compliance
Lightning Source LLC
LaVergne TN
LVHW051513070426
835507LV00022B/3089